LISTOWEL THROUGH A LENS

MARY COGAN

Listowel, Co. Kerry 2001 to 2009
Through the lens of Mary Cogan

Mary Cogan

ISBN   978-0-9563262-0-1

Printed and bound in Spain by
GraphyCems, Villatuerta, Navarra

Published in Ireland in 2009 by Crannsilini Publishing

Book Design by

ANDY O'DONOVAN
GRAPHIC DESIGN
andy@andyodonovan.ie

Introduction

"Photography has little to do with the things you see and everything to do with the way you see them." Elliott Erwitt.

This is not a photography book. It is merely a small piece of the history of Listowel and the story is told in my photographs.

I have for a long time been interested in taking photographs. I am a social photographer, recording a bit of family and local history.

In 2002 I went digital. My interest in documentary photography coincided with the coming of the economic boom to Listowel. I realised that the streetscapes of our town were changing almost daily. The prosperity that came with the Celtic Tiger era brought life and vibrancy to the town . New businesses sprang up like mushrooms, old businesses were invigorated and pursuits that we had never imagined could blossom into businesses were suddenly making a mint. I decided to do my best to chronicle this change.

Jim and I already had a personal webpage with a guide to places of interest in town. This was obviously the ideal place to display my photographs. We put an extra page onto the site called "The Changing Face of Listowel". This page generated a great deal of interest and I was encouraged to keep snapping.

Now I became a familiar sight on Listowel streets photographing everything that changed. Over time I built up a huge collection of photographs, a record of Listowel during the boom years.

By 2007 the global economy was taking a turn for the worst. In Ireland the property bubble burst and the flimsy framework on which the boom was constructed began to crumble. The face of Listowel began to change again. The big difference now was that when a business closed, no new business opened in its place. I realised that I had a photographic record of an era that was gone.

In response to urging from family and friends I decided to put the photographs into a book. Thus Listowel Through a Lens was born. The project then took on a life of its own. I decided to include other photographs I had taken of happy days in town.

The book does not aspire to be anything more than my own personal take on Listowel in the recent past. It is not comprehensive. I know that there is much that I have missed.

I dedicate the finished product, to an indulgent and hopefully not too critical audience of family, friends and Listowel neighbours.

Mary Cogan 2009

Index

Above is the Listowel branch of Kerry County Library, a modern building located in the plaza opposite Aras an Phiarsaigh and beside Listowel Courthouse.

On the next page, the Small Square is pictured in 2002 during the Nice Treaty referendum campaign. Listowel people had other things on their minds as well, as is evident in the posters.

The next picture is the entrance to the town from the Tralee side, with the Catholic presbytery on the left.
The third picture shows Lower William Street.

In the following pages you will see some well known public buildings.

Page 9, 10 & 11 show some aspects of town

Some Streetscapes

Listowel Castle is the finest of Listowel's public buildings. It stands beside The Seanchaí literary and heritage centre, hiding away in the corner of the town centre.

The bridges above lead to the racecourse.

Listowel is built on the river Feale. There are many fine bridges along the course of this river. "The Big Bridge" in Listowel is one of them. It is pictured here in April 2007.

Poor visibility on the day means that Kerry Ingredients is not visible in the background, so the bridge looks as it did centuries ago.

Changes

In the late nineties Listowel was still a rural market town. Shops ,with a few notable exceptions like McKennas and Carrolls, were small and owner occupied. The family usually lived over the shop. The streetscape was a mix of retail, residential and commercial property, with a sprinkling of derelict premises.

The 21st. century brought the birth of a new kind of entrepreneur, the property developer. He bought up shops and houses, refurbished them and then let them out to tenant shopkeepers. The old residents moved out to new homes in the country. These one-off mansions and housing estates were often developed on land that had previously been farmed.

Over time, most premises in town housed at least one shop. Irish people now bought houses in property shops, got money in mortgage shops and lots of unnecessary rubbish in "lifestyle shops". We lost the run of ourselves and there seemed no end to the ways enterprising shopkeepers could cash in on our rampant consumerism.

Services which did not need an on-street presence moved upstairs. The face of Listowel was changing almost daily. Sadly that rapid fire development has now slowed to a trickle and the cycle is now reversed. Again the face of Listowel is changing, with shop closures and businesses leaving town.

On the left are some Listowel sites which changed during the boom years. On pages 25-57 are some transformed premises. Some of these shops have changed hands, others merely had a face lift.

Changes

Changes

52

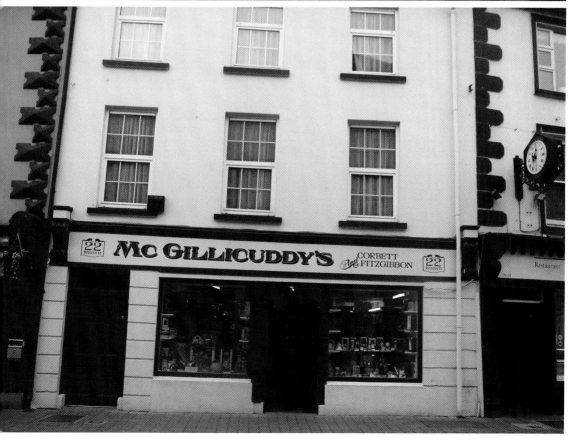

Above is a scene from the Garden of Europe.

In the foreground is The Holocaust memorial. This is four upright railway sleepers representing the railway lines that ferried so many to their deaths. The wood is held fast by iron chains and bars, symbols of captivity.

In the background is Patrick Tarrant's striking tribute to John B. Keane.

On the following pages are some other monuments and statues that adorn the town.

I EMBRACE MY MILLION BROTHERS
AND GREET THE WORLD WITH A KISS
KNOWING THAT OUR LOVING FATHER
DWELLS ABOVE THE STARS

Commissioned By
Jimmy Deenihan, Td
&
Listowel Rotary Club

Sculptor
Padraig Tarrant

John B Keane
1928 - 2002

Unveiled By Brenda Fricker
25th May, 2008

One of the big changes that took place in the last few years was the closing down of the convent and the convent chapel. This was followed by the departure of many of the
Presentation sisters from Listowel. It was a regrettable change that I never expected to see in my lifetime.

The convent which is a listed building was sold to a local consortium. The sale, however, fell through and this once lovely building is now falling into disrepair and ruin. After the closure of the convent an auction of the contents and fixtures took place in the convent chapel. The Stations of the Cross and statues found homes in nearby parishes. Other bits and bobs of the sisters' property were sold to the highest bidders. Many a Listowel home now treasures a souvenir of the nuns.

Convent

FOR SALE
Prime
Redevelopment
Opportunity
on approx. 1.4 Ha (3.5 acres)

GVA Donal O Buachalla

01 676 2711
www.gvadob.ie

AUCTION
MARSH
TEL: 021 27034

73

Above is Toirbheart. This building, up to 2008, housed the Family Centre. It was originally the Presentation School with the primary school on the ground floor and a secondary school upstairs.

It was later used as the infants' section of the girls' primary school before the whole girls' national school moved to the Ballybunion Road to a campus shared with the Nano Nagle School.

On the opposite page is Presentation Secondary School and St. Michael's College

Schools

Listowel has many symbols of its Catholic heritage on show. Here are a selection of grottos and Calvaries.

This Marian grotto is located in O'Connell's Avenue.

Our Lady of Fatima is in the secondary school car park.

Our Lady of Lourdes used to stand in her grotto in the corner of the convent garden.

There used to be a Calvary in the convent chapel grounds and there is a Calvary at Convent Cross.

The statue of St. Patrick dominates Upper William Street from its niche over St. Patrick's Hall.

St. Joseph stands in the hospital grounds.

The statue of Jesus carrying his cross is also in the hospital grounds.

WE ADORE THEE
O LORD JESUS CHRIST
AND WE BLESS THEE
BECAUSE BY
THY HOLY CROSS
THOU HAST REDEEMED
THE WORLD

The Lartigue Railway

The Lartigue monorail connected Listowel and Ballybunion from1888 to 1924. A life- size replica of this exotic mode of transport has been reconstructed near the original site. Since 2003, visitors and Listowel people can take a trip back in time on the short track, or view the Lartigue memorabilia in the nearby museum.

Famous People

I have managed to photograph some of the famous people who have visited Listowel over the past few years.

Above is Brenda Fricker who was in town to open the monument to John B. Keane in The Garden of Europe.

On the following pages are photos of President Mary McAleese who came to open the restored Lartigue.

Bertie Ahern came to open St. Michael's extension and his successor, Brian Cowen, came, in Summer 2008, to campaign for a "yes" vote in the Lisbon Treaty referendum.

Writers' Week brought poets Seamus Heaney and Roger McGough, actor Gabriel Byrne, and journalist Mary Kenny.

I photographed Niall Tóibín, John Sheehan, Maidhc Dainín OSé and the late Gary MacMahon at the unveiling of the John B. Keane statue in Main St. Micheal O Muircheartaigh launched Gaelscoil Lios Tuathail's commemorative journal in May 2009.

Christmas

Here are some scenes from Christmastime in town, the crib and Christmas tree in The Square, some decorated shop windows, the parish bazaar and pupils from Presentation Primary school carol singing.

Michael Dowling as St. Patrick leads out Listowel Emmets in the 2009 St Patrick's
Day parade. The following pages show scenes from previous years' parades.
As usual Dan Keane sits in judgement and John Lynch records it all, come hail,
rain or snow on the day.

The annual Corpus Christi procession takes place in June. The route varies from year to year.

Householders and business people along the chosen route decorate their windows with religious symbols and flags. Altars are erected at junctions along the way.

The priest carries the Eucharist in a monstrance. Local people take it in turns to carry the canopy that covers the priest. First communicants strew petals along the way.

The ceremony finishes with Benediction.

A regular feature of Fridays in Listowel is the Farmers' Market which takes place in the Square. While there are very few farmers, let alone country people, manning the stalls, there is a variety of produce available.

A colourful addition to Writers' Week and the annual food fair is an outdoor French Market. The Square is filled with the aromas of cheese, olives, crêpes and other French fare and, for one day only, a little corner of Listowel is transported to La Belle France.

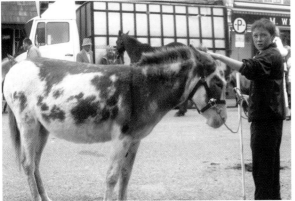

Every January I consult Old Moore's Almanac to see when the horse fairs are to be held in Listowel. Faithfully, I take my camera to record "the last horse fair".

So far I have gone through this ritual at least 6 times and still they go on for another year. The fair is now confined to Market Street and is carefully cordoned off and policed.

Above is a tack seller whom I photographed in 2005, one of the many colourful regulars at the fair.

It is my custom, when Jim and I are out walking, to ask anyone who stops to chat with Jim to pose for a photo. All of these photos would fill a book on their own so I have just included a representative few, and extend my apologies to people whose photo is left on the cutting room floor.
Above are some photos taken at The Races

Jim and friends

When does a week begin on a Wednesday evening and end on a Sunday?

When it's Writers' Week in Listowel, of course.

LWW is more than just a festival of writing. As well as workshops in various genres of writing, it features many different kinds of performance. There are book launches, readings, guided walks, a bus tour, live recordings, drama galore and many more delights in store for festival attendees.

The photo above is the view from the Square during the 30th Writers' Week in 2008.

When I talk of Listowel Races I mean the annual harvest festival of racing traditionally held in the last week of September. Once upon a time it held such a hallowed place in the local social calendar that the town seemed to me to hold its breath until "after The Races".

Schools and shops closed down for the week and everyone went to The Island. The streets came alive at night and everyone went to the pubs or "The Market". Nowadays the shops and schools carry on as normal, there is no Harvest Festival on the streets and the "rides" have decamped from the centre of town to The Cows' Lawn.

The Races still holds its place as the most important event in Listowel's year but it is now followed closely by Writers' Week, The Food Fair and other transitory festivals like Fleadh Cheoil na hEireann, and The Rás.

Above is a picture of the action on the track with a banner anticipating victory in the forthcoming All Ireland Football Final visible on the wall of the Listowel Arms in the background.

This group of musicians and volunteers took part in the annual M. S. Society busking day on June 5 2008.

Emmets football field was the venue for the band competitions at Fleadh Cheoil na hEireann in 2001. On the following pages are photos of the convent primary school marching band, the unveiling of the O'Rahilly memorial and the final of the Rás in 2006, the unveiling of the John B. sculpture in 2008 and the annual dog walk.

On May 15 2009 Scoil Realta na Maidine held a big event to officially open their new all weather playing area. A highlight of the day was the revival of old rivalries in a much anticipated town league match. The game was won by The Ashes who defeated An Gleann in the final. Above are the two teams captured before the match, and on the following pages are some local people whom I photographed on the day.

Listowel is famous for the unique plasterwork of the late Pat MacAuliffe. This craftwork and the beautiful shop fronts of the town are maintained by many firms of painters and signwriters.

My photo shows Fred Chute, a master painter and signwriter at work on one of Listowel's best known landmarks, The Harp and Lion.

Some signs are temporary like the ones ,top, which adorned the Small Square for a day in June 2008 and the ones ,above, in the same location for a short period in May 2009. Others are more lasting and add something to the story of the town. In the following pages I have a collection of some of the many signs, old and new, that adorn the streetscape of our town.

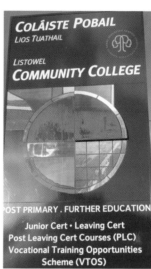

FEALE VALLEY
FITTED KITCHENS

www.fitzpatrickstravel.ie

ST. MICHAEL'S
COLLEGE

The Garden Of Europe

J.J. O'Quigley

GARDEN CENTRE
Florist AND
PET SHOP

DELICATESSEN
JOHN R's
HOME BAKERY
HOME COOKED MEATS, SALADS

Ionad Cathartha
CIVIC CENTRE

Carrchlós
PARKING P

Golf Club

Ospidéal
DISTRICT HOSPITAL

Clochar
CONVENT

Leithris Phoiblí
PUBLIC TOILETS

Cosán Sive
THE SIVE WALK

Paddypower.com

CHILDERS
PARK

'COWS LAWN'
PUBLIC PARK
SINCE LATE 60'S

GUINNESS
ST. JAMESS GATE WILLIAM St. LISTOWEL

LISTOWEL
ARMS HOTEL

ASSOCIATED WITH
DANIEL O'CONNELL
AND C.S. PARNELL

WRITERS GROVE

INAUGURATED BY
PRESIDENT MARY ROBINSON
MAY 24TH 1991
ROTARY CLUB OF LISTOWEL
AND LISTOWEL YOUTH CLUB

ALEXANDER SCHOLE PRESENTS
Australian Super Circus
SYDNEY
LISTOWEL
LISTOWEL RACE COURSE
FROM **FRIDAY 24TH APRIL** TO **SUNDAY 26TH APRIL**
ALL NEW SHOW
HEATED BIG TOP

RETREAT FOR MEN
... at ...
ARDFERT RETREAT CENTRE
... on ...
TUES. FEB 10th 8pm to 11pm
IF INTERESTED PLEASE CONTACT
Jack Mc Gillycuddy 'Corbetts'
22 William St. Listowel
068 - 21529
Timmy Griffin 068-40272
Michael Dillane 068-21596
Michael Dowling 068-21448

kevins
BAR FOOD
MORNING COFFEE
Hot Whiskey
Irish coffee
SANDWICHES
HOUSE SPECIAL
TOASTED
HAM CHEESE
& ONION
HAM * CHEESE
SALAD * BEEF
IRISH COFFEE SERVED

UDC | Comhairle Bhaile Cheantair Lios Tuathail
SAVE WASTE, FROM G OF THE GROUND | Le D'Thoil na fag aon cré/fuíollach, d bharr tochailte uaigh, sa Reilig

4th Annual
Patrick Griffin
Memorial Match
LISTOWEL CELTIC
Vs
BALLYGOLOGUE PARK
ON MONDAY 7th AUG. at 2pm, TANAVALLA
Man of the Match Award & Refreshments after at the New Kingdom Bar
Please come & Support

Have Fun! Feel Better!
LARTIGUE THEATRE
PRESENT
The White Headed Boy
BY LENNOX ROBINSON
AT
ST. JOHN'S, LISTOWEL
FRIDAY 23rd MARCH - WEDNESDAY 28th MARCH
NIGHTLY AT 8.00pm
Irish Comedy at its Best!
Book Early...Call 068-22566

TOM DUFFY'S CIRCUS
LISTOWEL
WEDS 4 & THURS 5 OCT
4.30 & 7.30

Store Closing
Friday 27th February at 5pm
The Management + Staff would like to thank all our customers for their support over the past year
Thank You.

Little Einsteins

Allo's
A Mother Is... A Mother of Memories
Mother's Day
Why not treat your Mother to Lunch in Allo's on her Special Day.
She's worth it!
Now taking Bookings

Sive
By John B. Keane
The Listowel Players
Monday 16th - Saturday 21st February 2009
St. John's The Square, Listowel
Booking Essential: 068 22566

PLAICE €15.50
COD €15.50
SALMON €14.50
TROUT €14.50
MONK €24.50
BLACK SOLE €16.50
LEMONS €15.50
JOHN DORY €EACH
HADDOCK €10.50
MACKEREL €9.50

ALLO'S
SEAFOOD BAR

P. B.
House
53 William St.
Listowel
Co. Kerry

CEARNÓG
DENTAL
SURGERY

MORKANS
JEWELLERS

JERRY & FIONA O'CONNOR
Number
7
PHARMACY & OPTICIAN
Market Street
Listowel

FINESSE
Bridal
Wear

KERRY DESIGN
Studio
K D S

HOME BAKERY • DELICATESSEN • FOOD HALL
John R's
COOKED MEATS · FINE WINES · CHEESE · SALADS

THE
Gold
CORNER

O'QUIGLEY
GENTS HAIRDRESSING
Since 1912

LOFTY'S

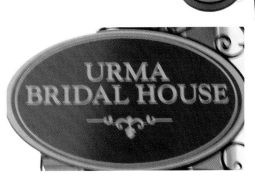

URMA
BRIDAL HOUSE

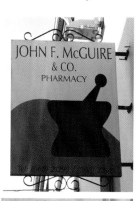

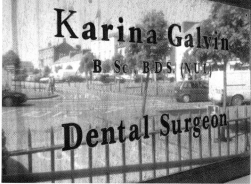

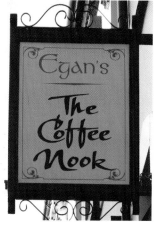

Post boxes in Listowel are an interesting mix of the old and the older. The box in the wall at Convent Cross and the pillar box at Leahy's Corner are relics from the era of British rule in Ireland and in Church Street there is a P&T post box.

Phone booths are set to disappear from our streets very shortly. Revenue from these had dwindled due to the widespread use of mobile phones.

It is a feature of Listowel that every premises has a back entrance. A network of back lanes, (known locally as back ways) connects the streets of the town, much in the manner of a rabbit warren.

Listowel was once like the Limerick described by Frank McCourt in Angela's Ashes with families living in crowded conditions in many of the houses in the lanes.
In the late 20th century the government introduced an urban renewal scheme. Grants and tax break incentives, including remission of rates, were offered to developers to invest in the regeneration of derelict and often unsightly areas in towns.
McKenna's yard had been sold some time previously to the L&N supermarket chain. This shop was later sold to Garvey's Super Valu. When Super Valu moved out, the building was bought by a local consortium and redeveloped to house the decentralised offices of The Revenue Commissioners.

Over time, other businesses opened up in the back lanes, although the urban renewal scheme was never as popular in Listowel as it was in other Irish towns. Today the landscape of the back lanes combines old stone lofts and stores, cheek by jowl with modern buildings. In the following pages you will see Old Mill Lane, Tae Lane, and lanes behind Church St. and William St.

In the last decade, retailing in Listowel has undergone a sea change. In the next section of the book is an account in pictures of the story of buying and selling in town. You will be amazed at how much has changed over a short few years. I have grouped shops into categories and I have included a mix of new and old.

The picture above was taken during the St. Patrick's Day parade in 2007 as a group of children wheelbarrowed the corpse of the Celtic Tiger through the streets. Evidence that he was purring his last was already visible .

When I came to Listowel first I was fascinated by the name of one local shop. It was called "The Fancy Warehouse". Even by the standards of the time it did not seem to me to be in any way fancy. In the recent past, however, every day we seemed to see fancier and fancier warehouses opening their doors. Art galleries opened. Listowel people wined and dined in greater numbers and in greater luxury than ever before. Computer shops and phones shops were added to the streetscape. Interior designers opened retail outlets. Hardware and furniture shops were busy. The rising tide was lifting all boats.

William St. has always had more than its fair share of gambling establishments. Small local turf accountant's shops have now given way to branches of large betting chains.

The local bookie's was once a dim uninviting place, frequented only by men. Betting shops are now big roomy and luxurious, providing armchairs and carpeted comfort to male and female punters. There were even snacks on offer during the week of Cheltenham !

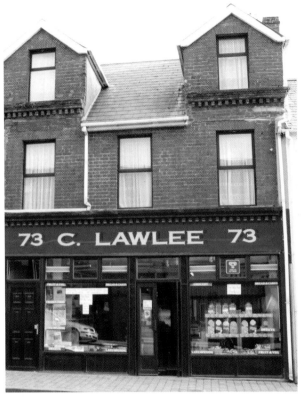

The small general grocery shop, like Carmel's is now a rarity. Big supermarkets and specialist shops are now the norm.

In the following pages I have supermarkets, a fish shop, butchers', convenience and forecourt stores.

John Griffin
Craft Butcher
Quality & Service
Second To None
Gourmet
Food
Hall

FISH SHOP
Ó Mathúna
SIOPA ÉISC

FRUIT & VEG

The Mermaids is Listowel's best known night club but for a few years that title was claimed by the club which used to be known as Cronins. It has been rebranded as Klub, Club C, Halo, Tonic, Exit and a few other names now lost to memory.

Video rental shops, once did great business. They have all now closed.

Kieran Gleeson's Classic Cineplex is still going strong

Gaelic football is still the preferred entertainment of most Listowel people.

Listowel has several fine veterinary practices. The Island Clinic has moved to St. Brendan's Terrace and Treacy Sheehan are about to relocate as well.

Our animals are certainly well looked after.

The Blue Umbrella was an artists' co-operative which sold artwork and various crafts. It was located in a shop, once Kenny Tobin butchers' and later Amazon Fashions.

Cada was a picture gallery in Carey's shop. It sold prints mainly and also provided a picture framing service.

Arkhangel was the Listowel outlet of a Limerick based gallery. It was located in a big airy premises in Church St. It displayed and sold work from a huge variety of artists. It relocated across the street for a short while before finally closing in 2008.

Olive Stack, a very successful local artist has her gallery and shop in Main St. and Brendan Landy operates Landyphoto.com from his premises in Charles St.

The Hannon family ran a newsagents from this shop in Main St. It sold books, newspapers, confectionery and souvenirs.

Nowadays we can buy our paper in the supermarket but shops like Robert Moloney's, O'Donovan's, Flavin's and Hannon's were primarily paper shops in the traditional sense.

The Kerryman office was located in Main St. The Advertiser started out in an office at the corner of Church St. and Courthouse Road in a shop that housed Crowley's sweet shop when I first came to Listowel. Peter McGuire had a stationery shop in Church St. for a while.

Listowel Printing Works occupies a central location in Church St., Rapid Print is now closed and Tulsa Gleeson's In Print operates from 52a Church St.

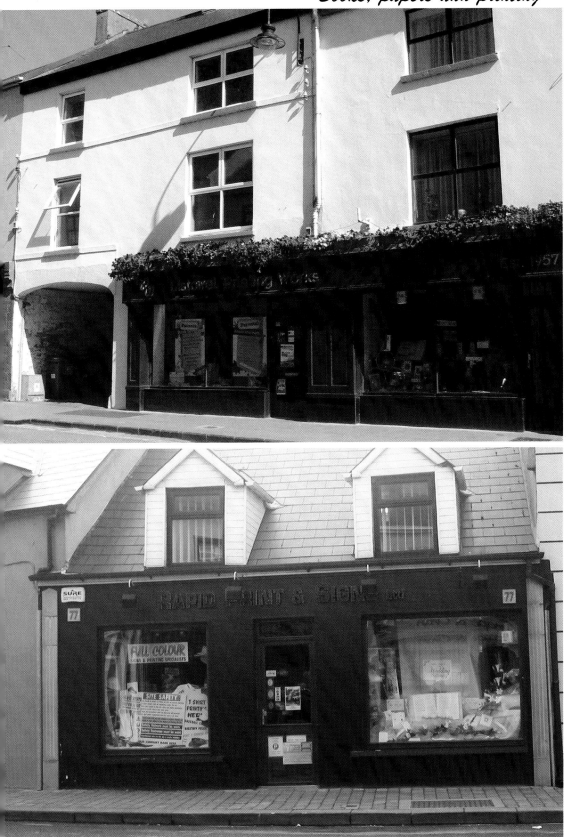

Books, papers and printing

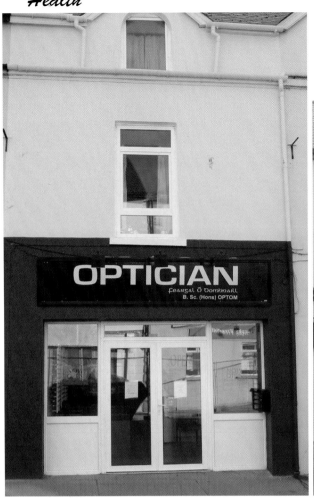

Courthouse Rd. houses both a doctor's and a dentist's surgeries.
The picturesqe Ivy Clinic is located in The Square.
In the following pages are some of the buildings in town with some kind of
health connection.

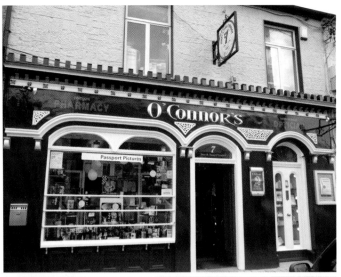

Five pharmacies serve the people of Listowel.. Maguire's ,above, opens on to Church St. and Main St.

There was a time when every second shop in town seemed to have a licence to sell alcohol. That changed gradually as these licences began to change hands for big money. At one time, in order to sell alcohol in a new premises one had to buy two existing licences. Supermarkets now opened off licence departments and the small grocery shop cum pub became a thing of the past.

In the early part of the twenty first century pubs did a roaring trade. Driving through town on a Saturday night I was always amazed by the numbers of people pouring out of Chutes Bar and crossing the road to The Maid of Erin in the hope that it would be less crowded. Both of these bars are now closed.

Several factors, including the introduction of the smoking ban, increases in the price of alcohol and the global recession have put paid to the glory days of the licenced trade.

In the following pages I have included some hostelries which have weathered the storms and some that have succumbed to the rough winds of change.

Places to drink

The Listowel Arms Hotel has many historical associations. Parnell is said to have stayed there. It was owned for a time by the tenor, Josef Locke. It is now run by the O'Callaghan family.

In these pages I have gathered together restaurants, like Allo's in its old and its new guise, coffee shops, gastro pubs, fast food and ethnic restaurants. I have included a few eating houses that are now closed.

One premises, once Slemon's Shoe Shop has seen many changes, Roma, Pronto a Mangiar, Oscar Wilde's, Europe and now Off The Square Café.

Meals to eat at home can be bought in many of these restaurants.

Places to eat

186

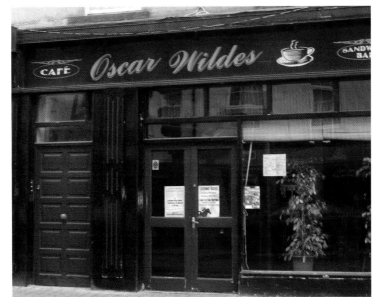

Places to eat

This category is very loosely titled. I have put into these following pages shops which sell all kinds of things for the home. I have included flower shops, and shops which cater for hobbies like music or fishing. Many of these shops were casualties of the economic downturn.

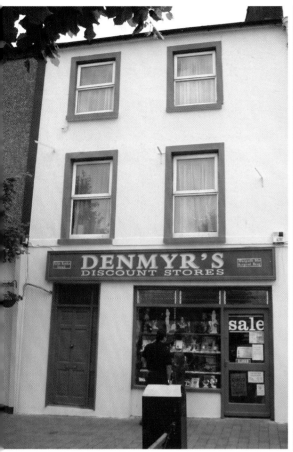

McKenna's and Carrolls are the two big family owned hardware businesses in Listowel. Both of these companies have a shop and a yard.

Stack's Arcade and Pat Nolan's sell furniture and floor covering.

I have included in this section shops which loosely come under the heading of hardware.

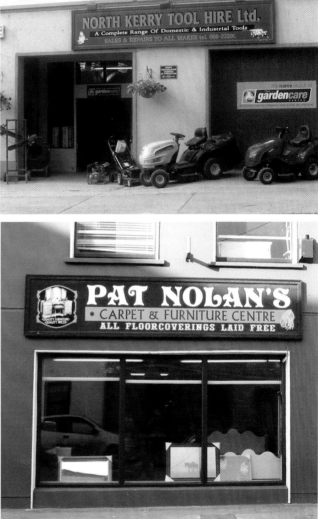

Personal grooming was a huge industry during affluent times. In the good years we saw a huge increase in the popularity of a phenomenon called "pampering". This involved not only hair care but all sorts of treatments for face, body and nails. In the following pages are some of the places where you could avail of these treatments.

203

Morkan's is the longest established of Listowel's jewellery shops. During the boom years there was an increased demand for items which became known as "Bling". Shops like Suzanne's and X-tension opened to serve this market.

Pharmacies and other shops added costume jewellery to their range of products.

This market has contracted greatly in the recession.

For a while, I.T. & phone shops seemed to appear overnight. Demand for all sorts of technological gadgets rocketed. Mobile phones had to be upgraded regularly in order to keep pace with developments. No sooner had you taken it out of the box than your computer was out of date.

Traditionally, banks occupied big solid imposing buildings. This was meant to inspire confidence. During the boom in Ireland, several new banks came into the country. We had lots of money so there grew an industry in money advice, money lending, and schemes to help us save or invest this cash that we had in plenty. In the following pages I have included banks, the Credit Union, building societies and mortgage shops.

After the money pages I have the property shops. Auctioneers no longer worked from offices in back rooms. They now had a presence on the high street with windows full of photographs of properties for sale or rent. Very often the real estate shop was next door to the mortgage lender. There you could get the loan to buy the starter home, the buy-to-rent apartment, or even the holiday villa in the sun.

Everyone who was anyone owned property in Bulgaria.

215

General Drapers like Moriarty's were once two a penny in Listowel. Now clothes shops specialise in one sector of the clothes' market.

Trades like tailoring and dressmaking are long gone from our streets. Nowadays Listowel has a name for exclusive boutiques selling unusual as well as well-known brands. The town is also a popular shopping venue for the bride- to- be and wedding guests. There are two bridal boutiques, a milliner and numerous dress shops in town.

I have divided the following pages roughly into men's, women's and children's fashions.

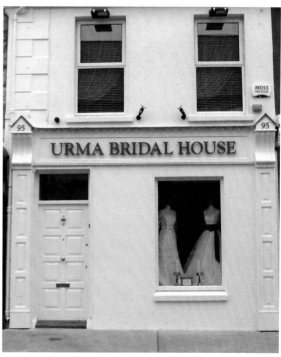

Page by page guide to the pictures:

This brave little robin sums up a lot of what the book is about. I photographed him perched on a shopping trolley at Lidl.

A robin is territorial and will defend his patch against all comers. For me he symbolises the old order holding out gamely against the new.

Listowel has changed much in the past few years but the old values of friendship and honesty are still at its core.